First World War
and Army of Occupation
War Diary
France, Belgium and Germany

57 DIVISION
170 Infantry Brigade
King's Own (Royal Lancaster Regiment)
2/5th Battalion
8 September 1915 - 29 February 1916

WO95/2979/6

The Naval & Military Press Ltd
www.nmarchive.com
Published in association with The National Archives

Published by

The Naval & Military Press Ltd

Unit 10 Ridgewood Industrial Park,

Uckfield, East Sussex,

TN22 5QE England

Tel: +44 (0) 1825 749494

www.naval-military-press.com

www.nmarchive.com

This diary has been reprinted in facsimile from the original. Any imperfections are inevitably reproduced and the quality may fall short of modern type and cartographic standards.

© **Crown Copyright**
Images reproduced by permission of The National Archives, London, England, 2015.

Contents

Document type	Place/Title	Date From	Date To
Heading	WO95/2979/6		
Heading	57 Div 170 Bde 2/5 KO R Lancaster Regt 1915 Aug-1916 Feb		
Miscellaneous	Statement August 1915		
Heading	War Diary Of The 2/5th Bn. Royal Lancaster Regt. For The Month Of September 1915		
War Diary		08/09/1915	28/09/1915
Heading	War Diary Of The 2/5th Bn The Kings Own R.L.R. From 1st October 1915 To 30th October 1915		
War Diary		01/10/1915	30/10/1915
Heading	2/5th Bn The Kings Own R.L. Regt. War Diary For November 1915		
War Diary	Ashford	05/11/1915	29/11/1915
Heading	2/5th Bn The Kings Own RL Regt War Diary For December 1915		
War Diary	Ashford	03/12/1915	30/12/1915
Heading	War Diary Of 2/5th Bn. The Kings Own R.L. Regt. For January 1916		
War Diary	Ashford	01/01/1916	31/01/1916
Heading	War Diary Of The 2/5th Bn The Kings Own R.L. Regt.		
War Diary		01/02/1916	29/02/1916

57 DIV

170 BDE

2/5 K O R LANCASTER REGT

1915 AUG — 1916 FEB

Index

SUBJECT.

Overseas Forces: Week ending -

No.	Contents.	Date.
	April 22nd	
	" 29th	
	May 6th	
	" 13th	
	" 20th	
	" 27th	
	June 17th	

Statement.
August, 1915.

Unit:- 2/5th. The King's Own. Royal Lancaster Regt.
Brigade:- 170th Infantry Brigade.
Division:- 57th (West Lancs) Division
Temporary War Station:- Ashford. Kent.
Stations since occupied subsequent to concentration:-
Blackpool. Sevenoaks. Tandridge Camp (Surrey).

(a). Mobilization: no remarks.
(b). Concentration at War Stations. no remarks
(c) Organization for defence: Considerably below strength since the separation of the Home Service men into a separate unit.
(d). Training: The whole battalion is trained except 152, & all ~~have~~ have fired the general Musketry course except 152.
(e). Discipline: Good.
(f). Administration: Suffering from shortage of senior Officers.
(g). Reorganization of T.F. Units home & imperial service units: 104 rank & file arrived from the 41st Provisional Battn on Aug 6th 1915.
(h). Preparation of unit for Imperial Service. Trained except the 152 mentioned above, but short of senior officers & of men.

H. Seward Capt
Commanding 2/5 The King's Own
R Lanc Regt

CONFIDENTIAL.

WAR DIARY.

of the

1/5th Bn. Royal Lancaster Regt.

for the month of SEPTEMBER, 1915.

To BdE

Army Form C. 2118.

WAR DIARY
INTELLIGENCE SUMMARY

2/5th The King's Own (R. Lan. R.)

(Erase heading not required.)

Hour, Date, Place	Summary of Events and Information	Remarks and references to Appendices
1915. September 8th	150 N.C.O.'s & men proceeded under the command of 2nd Lieut. H. Critchley to Sandwich to join 256 Musketry Course.	
9th	C.S.M.I. Brown, I.M. proceeded to join the 1/5th Battn. The King's Own (R. Lan. R.) overseas.	
14th	Lieut-Colonel J.W. Sharpe reported his arrival & assumed command of the Battalion from this date.	
20th	Transport inspected by O.C. 57th West Lancs. Divisional Train.	
28th	Battalion inspected by Col. S.H. Harrison, commanding the 170th Infantry Brigade, in Hatch Park. 2nd Lieuts Ruddell & Russell + 60 N.C.O.'s & men proceeded to Bilsington, + 2nd Lt. Cathy & Gillespie + 60 N.C.O.'s & men returned from Bilsington.	

Ashford
4/10/15

Sharpe COLONEL
O.C. 2/5th BN. THE KING'S OWN R. LANCASTER REGT

CONFIDENTIAL.

WAR DIARY.
— of —
The 2/5th Bn The King's Own. R.L.R.

From. 1st October 1915 / to 30th October. 1915.

Army Form C. 2118.

THE KING'S OWN ROYAL LANCASTER REGT

WAR DIARY

~~INTELLIGENCE SUMMARY~~

(Erase heading not required.)

Instructions regarding War Diaries and Intelligence Summaries are contained in F.S. Regs., Part II. and the Staff Manual respectively. Title pages will be prepared in manuscript.

Hour, Date, Place	Summary of Events and Information	Remarks and references to Appendices
Oct. 1st. 1915.	Inspection of the Brigade by Major General G.J. Sorsle Commanding 59th (West Lancs) Divsn.	
" 2nd.	The Exchange of Companies on working party at BILSINGTON completed.	
" 6th.	Detached Working Party at BILSINGTON recalled to Station	
" 7th.	Lecture to all Officers and Transport men by Capt. Walker A.V.C.(?) subject "Horses & Stable Management".	
" 9th.	O.C's Inspection of the Battalion bands.	
" 13th.	Inspection of the Battn by the A.Q.M.G. & Munition Officers	
" 27th.	Lecture to all Officers and Transport men by the M. Clarke R.S.P.C.A subject "Horsemanship".	
" 30th.	Inspection of the music Vic by the Brigadier in Divisional Parade.	

G. Sharpe
COLONEL
C.O. 2/5th BN. THE KING'S OWN R. LANCASTER REGT

CONFIDENTIAL.

2/5th Bn The King's Own. R. L. Regt.

War Diary
for
NOVEMBER 1915.

Ashford.   December 18th 1915

WAR DIARY
INTELLIGENCE SUMMARY
(Erase heading not required.)

Army Form C. 2118.

Instructions regarding War Diaries and Intelligence Summaries are contained in F.S. Regs., Part II. and the Staff Manual respectively. Title pages will be prepared in manuscript.

Hour, Date, Place	Summary of Events and Information	Remarks and references to Appendices
Ashford 3rd November	2nd Lieuts Critchley & Bennett left Ashford to proceed overseas as reinforcement to 1/5th Bn.	Fid.
18th "	Inspection of Regimental Transport by D.A.Q.M.G.	Fid. Complimented on Transport.
18th "	1/5th (Mid.) Lancs Division.	Price.
19th "	Inspection of Regt. Transport by Major General F.W.B. Fus. Landon – (Fore-noon)	
19th "	Inspection of Regt. Transport by the Inspector of Fid. Remounts – (Afternoon)	
21st "	Inspection of Battalion by Major General Bt. Duckworth. Recommended more time be Inspector of Infantry at Hatch Park.	devoted to Coy training.
27th "	2 Officers and 75 men proceeded to Tenterden to relieve the 2/2nd West Kent Cyclists – Duty – Coast Defence Patrol.	Fid.
29th "	Inspection of Transport by O.C. No 2 Coy West Lancashire Divisional Train. A.S.C. in Edwards Road.	Fid.

Shoeing & boots = Good
Co:idition of mules, Harness & Men
Harness = V. Good
Vehicles = Fair
Shoeing = Fair

Guthrie
COLONEL
O.C. 2/5th BN. THE KING'S OWN R. LANCAST[ER]

CONFIDENTIAL   1/5th Bn The King's Own R.L Regt

War Diary
for December 1915

Ashford.

Army Form C. 2118.

WAR DIARY
INTELLIGENCE SUMMARY
(Erase heading not required.)

Instructions regarding War Diaries and Intelligence Summaries are contained in F. S. Regs., Part II. and the Staff Manual respectively. Title pages will be prepared in manuscript.

Hour, Date, Place	Summary of Events and Information	Remarks and references to Appendices
Ashford.		
Friday 3rd December 1915	Inspection of Books and Correspondence of the bn. at the Battalion Headquarters by G.O.C. 57th West Lancashire Division	W.H.H.
4th December 1915	Inspection of Guard Reports and Correspondence by Colonel S.H. Harrison Commanding 170th Infantry Brigade.	W.H.H.
20th December 1915	Inspection by Superintendent of Gymnasia at Hatch Park in Bayonet Fighting and Physical Drill	W.H.H.
29th December 1915	Inspection of one Company in Musketry on the Miniature Range by the Commandant School of Musketry, Hythe.	W.H.H.
30th December 1915	Regimental Transport inspected by O.C. No 2 Company West Lancashire Division Train A.S.C.	W.H.H.

Stockavon Lt Colonel
Commanding 2/5 The King's Own R.L.R.

CONFIDENTIAL

War Diary

- of -

2/5th Bn The King's Own R.L. Regt.

- for -

January 1916.

Ashford
Feby 3/16.

Army Form C. 2118.

WAR DIARY
~~INTELLIGENCE SUMMARY~~

(Erase heading not required.)

Instructions regarding War Diaries and Intelligence Summaries are contained in F. S. Regs., Part II. and the Staff Manual respectively. Title pages will be prepared in manuscript.

Hour, Date, Place	Summary of Events and Information	Remarks and references to Appendices
Ashford, January 1st 1915	- NIL -	Fol.
2nd	- NIL -	Fol.
3rd	- NIL -	Fol.
4th	- NIL -	Fol.
5th	- NIL -	Fol.
6th	- NIL -	Fol.
7th	- NIL -	Fol.
8th	- NIL -	Fol.
9th	- NIL -	Fol.
10th	- NIL -	Fol.

Army Form C. 2118.

WAR DIARY
INTELLIGENCE SUMMARY
(Erase heading not required.)

Instructions regarding War Diaries and Intelligence Summaries are contained in F. S. Regs., Part II. and the Staff Manual respectively. Title pages will be prepared in manuscript.

Hour, Date, Place	Summary of Events and Information	Remarks and references to Appendices
Ashford. January 11th	- NIL -	F.H.
12th	- NIL -	F.H.
13th	Inspection of Battalion by Commander II Army Central Force.	F.H.
14th	- NIL -	F.H.
15th	- NIL -	F.H.
16th	- NIL -	F.H.
17th	- NIL -	F.H.
18th	- NIL -	F.H.
19th	- NIL -	F.H.
20th	- NIL -	F.H.

Army Form C. 2118.

WAR DIARY

~~INTELLIGENCE SUMMARY~~

(Erase heading not required.)

Instructions regarding War Diaries and Intelligence Summaries are contained in F. S. Regs.; Part II. and the Staff Manual respectively. Title pages will be prepared in manuscript.

Hour, Date, Place	Summary of Events and Information	Remarks and references to Appendices
Ashford January 1st 1916	- NIL -	7.1.7.
2nd	- NIL -	7.1.7.
3rd	- NIL -	7.1.7.
4th	Brigade Tire Alarm.	
5th	- NIL -	7.1.7.
6th	- NIL -	7.1.7.
7th	- NIL -	7.1.7.
8th	Inspection of Regimental Transport by O.C. 106th Bn. Transport London A.S.C. and line transport by Brigadier Inspection of Battalion and machine gun section commanding 106th Infantry Brigade.	7.1.7.
9th	Arrival of 3 more commanders.	7.1.7.

Army Form C. 2118.

WAR DIARY

~~INTELLIGENCE SUMMARY~~

(Erase heading not required.)

Instructions regarding War Diaries and Intelligence Summaries are contained in F. S. Regs., Part II. and the Staff Manual respectively. Title pages will be prepared in manuscript.

Hour, Date, Place	Summary of Events and Information	Remarks and references to Appendices
Ashford. January 30th.	- NIL -	7th.
31st.	- NIL -	8th.

J. Sutherne
COLONEL
O.C. 2/5th Bn. THE KING'S OWN R. LANCASTER REGT.

War Diary

- of the -

2/5th Bn. The King's Own. R.L. Regt.

Ashford
February 1916.

Army Form C. 2118.

WAR DIARY
INTELLIGENCE SUMMARY

(Erase heading not required.)

Instructions regarding War Diaries and Intelligence Summaries are contained in F. S. Regs., Part II. and the Staff Manual respectively. Title pages will be prepared in manuscript.

Hour, Date, Place	Summary of Events and Information	Remarks and references to Appendices
1916		
February		
1st	Nil	Nil
2nd	Nil	Nil
3rd	Nil	Nil
4th	Nil	Nil
5th	Nil	Nil
6th	Observation Post at Loring furnished by this unit been withdrawn	Nil
7th	Nil	Nil
8th	Nil	Nil
9th	Nil	Nil
10th	Nil	Nil
11th	Nil	Nil
12th	Nil	Nil
13th	Nil	Nil
14th	Nil	Nil
15th	Nil	Nil
16th	Nil	Nil
17th	Nil	Nil
18th	Nil	Nil
19th	Nil	Nil
20th	Nil	Nil
21st	Nil	Nil
22nd	Nil	Nil
23rd	Received Operation Order No 1 at 5:55 p.m.	Nil
24th	Nil	Nil
25th	Nil	Nil
26th	Nil	Nil
27th	Nil	Nil
28th	Nil	Nil
29th	Nil	Nil

Sudbury Lt Col.
Commanding 2/5 The King's Own R.L.R.

www.ingramcontent.com/pod-product-compliance
Lightning Source LLC
Chambersburg PA
CBHW081509160426
43193CB00014B/2632